Presented to:

_____

From:

_____

Date:

_____

DEVOTIONS
FOR
Easter

Written and Compiled by Stacy J. Edwards

ZONDERVAN®

ZONDERVAN

Devotions for Easter

Copyright © 2017 by Zondervan

Requests for information should be addressed to:

Zondervan, 3900 Sparks Dr., SE, Grand Rapids, MI 49546

ISBN 978-0-310-35949-4

Cover design: Brand Navigation

Cover illustration: iStock/alexeikadirov

Interior illustration: Shutterstock

Interior design: Mallory Collins

Printed in China

17 18 19 20 21 22 /TIMS/ 9 8 7 6 5 4 3 2 1

Contents

Introduction

Growing up, holidays were always a big deal in my house, and they included everything a holiday should: decorations, good food, and lots of family. My favorite part of it all was that anytime my parents and their siblings got together, someone was going to tell a story. Sure, it would probably be the same story that someone else told the year before. There might be a squabble over the details, but none of that mattered. I would still laugh at the same parts and feign surprise at the way it turned out. Those stories are a huge part of who I am today.

I always tell people that I am many things: a Christ-chaser, a pastor's wife, a trucker's daughter, an author, and a homeschooling mother to five daughters. I have also *always* been a sucker for a good story. Whether they were my grandfather's war stories, my dad's over-the-road trucker stories, or my mother's mesmerizing account of an angel carrying her baby sister to heaven, I

learned early on that stories make a difference. Stories enable us to feel close to family members we've never met, learn from mistakes we didn't have to make, and witness God's faithfulness throughout the years—and *the best ones* are the ones that are told over and over again.

The children of Israel were instructed on several occasions to share their stories with their own children. The psalmist made it clear that God's people were to share His faithfulness so that future generations would hear the stories and pass them on to their children (Psalm 78:5–6). It's why, as the people crossed over the Jordan, they were told to pick up a stone. Then, when future children asked what those stones meant, the people were to tell their story (Joshua 4:6–7). It was always God's intention that we be a storytelling people.

With that in mind, I invite you to join me as I share some of my favorite Easter stories from history, from Scripture, and from my personal collection of family stories. My prayer is that as we make our way closer to Easter, these stories will serve to point us all to the greatest story ever told. Let's journey to the cross together.

—STACY J. EDWARDS

DAY 1

No Turning Back

*The crowds that went ahead of him and those that
followed shouted, "Hosanna to the Son of David!"*
—MATTHEW 21:9

*H*ave you ever had a "no turning back" kind of moment? There's no mistaking it when it happens. A feeling deep inside tells you that from this point forward, things will never be the same. It could have been the birth of a child or the loss of a loved one. Maybe it was a moment when you were presented with two career options, or when you made a decision about a relationship. Can you recall the feelings that accompanied that kind of moment?

For me, that moment came on Easter Sunday, 1984. There, in the pew of Alliance Baptist Temple, God lit a fire in my heart that still burns bright today. A realization of my desperate need, a plea for forgiveness, and a determination to walk in a new life all set me on a path of no return.

And Palm Sunday represented such a moment in Jesus' life. This is the day we celebrate Jesus' triumphal entry into Jerusalem.

As He entered the city, the crowds shouted, "Hosanna!" and declared Him King. *This*, Bible scholars tell us, *this moment* was Jesus' "no turning back" moment. He "crossed the point of no return," for those in power simply could not allow Him to continue challenging their authority as He had.[1]

Can you imagine the intensity of that moment? Jesus' entire earthly ministry had been leading Him to this precise point. Every miracle performed and every message preached had been in preparation for this day. The Pharisees and government officials may have previously backed down or overlooked other perceived offenses, but not this one. They could not. In the midst of the celebratory atmosphere, tension hung in the air; there would be consequences.

Jesus sealed His fate when He rode into Jerusalem that day. He didn't cloak His identity in parables or hidden messages; He declared Himself to be *the* Messiah. An action like that could not be undone. The time had come for Him to reveal Himself, ensuring that His death would come soon. Jesus knew this, yet He did not cower, back down, or change His mind. His love for us carried Him straight to the cross.

As you contemplate Easter and what it means for you,

allow yourself to follow in His steps. Hear the shouting of the crowds. Look into the faces of those who loved Him. Consider the incredible weight that must have rested on His shoulders. What kind of love must have kept Him going—to the point of "no turning back"—knowing He would soon be despised and crucified? Take in every word of His final teachings. May your love and gratitude for Him carry you straight to the cross. No turning back.

Thank You, Lord, for marching *bravely* to the cross. You never looked back. Give me that same *determination*, and help me follow You with every step.

DAY 2

At the Easter Parade

"Be careful not to practice your righteousness in front of others to be seen by them. If you do, you will have no reward from your Father in heaven."

—Matthew 6:1

If you use social media this Easter Sunday, you'll see (and perhaps post) snaps of immaculate, pastel-colored outfits, well-groomed children, and spring foliage. Then there's the fine china at Easter lunch, the glistening ham, the table settings, and flowers. It's a veritable online Easter parade!

The Easter parade is nothing new, of course. In fact, things were not all that different before the Internet, though the venue has certainly changed. Easter parades have been a fixture in New York City since the mid-1800s. Society's elite would first attend the morning church service and then would parade around the town to be seen by all in their Easter finery. The Easter parade was all about being seen and admired.

The biggest difference these days, though, is in the personal details we can add to our online parade. Aside from splendid

pictures, we're tempted to announce our charitable causes, what we're giving up for Lent, and anything we're particularly proud of. But what are our motives? Are we in danger of letting this holy holiday become all about being seen and admired?

The Pharisees were known for making this mistake. They loved the limelight, and they constantly put themselves and their righteousness on display—especially on holy days. But Jesus gave very clear instructions on how we are to conduct our spiritual activities. Whether it's worship, celebration, prayer, fasting, or giving to the poor, we should never do anything in an attention-seeking manner. In fact, if you reach out to give an offering, Jesus said, you shouldn't even let your left hand know what your right hand is doing (Matthew 6:3)! Now that's quite different from how the world would have us behave, isn't it?

This Easter season, be intentional about not making a production. Choose to be sincere instead of flashy. If no one knows how often we pray or how much we gave to the local food bank, it's okay. We don't need to send out a mass message letting folks know that we'll be giving up coffee for forty days. We can honor the Lord by doing all these things in secret, knowing that the Father who sees what's done in secret will reward us.

Help me let go of the need to be seen and *admired*, Lord. Remind me that You see and *reward* the things done in secret.

DAY 3

Thet Thing

*After fasting forty days and
forty nights, he was hungry.*
—MATTHEW 4:2

What comforts you? What is that *thing* that you automatically turn to for relaxation after a particularly hard day? Some of us find solace in a hot cup of coffee. Others, perhaps, lose themselves in television or a good book. It could even be a person to whom you look for validation. Maybe, for you, it's food. After all, a piece of cheesecake never hurt anyone's feelings. The reality is that we all have something that we use to try to soothe our wounds and bolster our strength.

Lent is a time when many Christians choose to deny themselves that *thing* and, instead, focus on prayer or another spiritual discipline. For instance, rather than reaching for your morning cup of tea, reach for your Bible. Instead of spending time watching your favorite television show, you might listen to worship music or have a time of prayer. It's common for people to fast from social media or sugary desserts. The point? To let go of an earthly comfort in order to cling all the more to the Lord.

Prior to being tempted by Satan, Jesus spent forty days and forty nights fasting. In His day *fasting* would have meant a denial of food. So it's understandable that Jesus felt very hungry at the end of the fast. Satan might have thought this would make Jesus weak, but not so. By denying Himself physical nourishment and dedicating Himself instead to spiritual nourishment, Jesus was better equipped to handle the Devil's temptations. So when the time came to face the Enemy, Jesus was filled with Scripture, which He used to shield Himself against Satan's attacks.

So . . . could it be that hunger is good for us? The psalmist declared that the Lord fills the hungry soul with good things (Psalm 107:9). When we enter God's presence hungry, we are putting ourselves in a position to be filled. Why then do we tend to fear spiritual hunger? At the first hint of that empty ache, we reach for something to fill it. And the world offers up a smorgasbord of choices which, while not all bad, are usually not best. But if we train ourselves to take that emptiness and fill it with God, our needs will be satisfied by His loving generosity.

That brings us back to *that thing*. What is it that God may be asking you to let go of for a time in order to be filled with the good things only He can provide? Enter His presence hungry, and allow Him to fill you with good things.

DAY 4

Sunday Best

*Peter took him aside and began to
rebuke him. "Never, Lord!" he said.
"This shall never happen to you!"*
—MATTHEW 16:22

What do you consider your "Sunday best"? Do those words call up images of flouncy childhood outfits with layers, lace, pastels, or patent leather shoes? These clothes made for lovely photos but caused an awful lot of pinching, chafing, and restless wiggles in the pews. These days, we seem to have gravitated toward a more comfortable way of dressing for church. This is not necessarily a bad thing (especially for those poor kids!). But it does remind us of our human impulse to seek more and more comfort in every area of life: physically, emotionally, financially, and spiritually. We might even attempt to create a comfortable Christianity, overlooking those ideas that make us flinch. The only problem is that there is nothing comfortable about the cross.

The idea of a suffering Savior made the apostle Peter positively chafe. Peter acknowledged that Jesus was the Christ

(Matthew 16:16) but balked at the idea of His death. He wanted Him to take the words back. He rebuked Him. This wasn't what he expected. Christ's teaching, healing, miracles—Peter was comfortable with those scenarios. But, now, He was talking about death. There was nothing comfortable about following Him to a grave.

If we are honest, we are probably not that different from Peter. Those of us who are Christ-followers are quick to call Him Lord, but what about when God's plan goes outside our comfort zone? Are we willing to go to that place, minister to those people, adopt that child, give up that thing we know we should?

We do not have to be slaves to our desire for comfort. Let's choose to put ourselves in situations that require us to lean fully on God's provision. Today, let's put Christ ahead of our comfort, as He put us ahead of His.

DAY 5

Pancake Day

*Jesus went with his disciples to a place
called Gethsemane, and he said to them,
"Sit here while I go over there and pray."*
—MATTHEW 26:36

The day before Lent begins is known by several names.
The official name is Shrove Tuesday, but some refer to it
as Fat Tuesday or Mardi Gras. Another name, and my personal
favorite, is Pancake Day. Admit it: pancakes make practically
everything sound better, don't they? Can you think of any scenario that could not be made just a little bit more enjoyable by a
nice stack of pecan pancakes?

Shrove Tuesday was meant to serve as a reminder that the
season of Lent was about to begin. Historically, during Lent,
Christians would abstain from things such as butter, cheese, and
fat—all the good stuff! Fat Tuesday became a time for people to
indulge in these things, and meals often featured pancakes. They
would fill themselves with the rich, sweet treat before entering
a season of self-denial and penance. After all, when you know
what is coming, it's nice to be able to plan ahead.

When Jesus was about to enter the final season of His earthly ministry, He prepared by retreating to Gethsemane for a time of prayer. Knowing He was about to give everything He had and completely empty Himself, He took time to step away and be with the Father. How God must have filled His Son with peace, comfort, and everything He would need to make it through the coming days.

We don't always have the luxury of knowing when a difficult season lies ahead of us. We have all had days when we wake up to life as usual but go to bed that evening with everything changed, the rug pulled out from under us. In those moments all we have to go on is what we have already chosen to fill ourselves with. If we have gorged ourselves on the things of the world, our resources will be quickly depleted. But if we have been intentional about filling ourselves with the things of God, we will have a store of peace and strength that is more than enough.

Ask God to fill you with Himself each day. The psalmist declares that the Lord will satisfy the thirsty and will fill the hungry with good things (Psalm 107:9). Who doesn't want good things? And if those good things happen to include pancakes with pure maple syrup, well, that's quite all right with me.

DAY 6

Straight to the Cross

As the time approached for him to be taken up to heaven, Jesus resolutely set out for Jerusalem.

—LUKE 9:51

Distraction is something we all deal with. You may remember having a dream, calling, or perhaps an inkling of what God created you to do. Then along came jobs, bills, dental appointments, and everything in between. Before you know it, you're just trying to make it to bedtime so you can get some sleep, get up, and do it all over again.

But what if we could separate ourselves from all the distractions and focus on what really matters? Can you think of the last time you gave your complete and undivided attention to something important, laying aside all distractions?

Brother Glenn knew how to keep his eyes fixed on what mattered. He came from a small town in southern Alabama and ended up pastoring a very successful church with several thousand members in middle Tennessee. He was the kind of preacher you would listen to with your pen at the ready because you knew he was going to say something worth writing down.

Folks often asked him how he could come up with fresh material week after week, year after year. Brother Glenn would respond by saying, "It's not that difficult. I just take any passage of Scripture and run to the cross." He wasn't distracted by trying to entertain people. Instead, he kept his eyes on the cross and the message of Scripture, and God was glorified.

When the time came for Jesus to begin His journey to the cross, He didn't allow any distractions to stop Him. The cross was His God-given task, and He would have nothing to do with any attempts to alter His course. When Peter dared to chastise Jesus for speaking of His death, Jesus stopped him short. "Get behind me, Satan," He demanded. Peter was being a hindrance to what had to take place (Matthew 16:23). Jesus was on His way to the cross, and He would not be distracted.

Do you have that kind of commitment to God's will? Are you faithful in the easy times but a bit more distracted when things get tough or even just busy? When you're beset by distraction, ask yourself one question: What are you focusing on? Or, more importantly, what God-glorifying things are you being distracted from? Let go of anything that is not leading you straight to the cross and the hope it holds.

Lead me to Your *cross*, Lord.
Teach me to *recognize* and set
aside those things that serve
only to *distract* me from You.

DAY 7

The Old
Rugged Cross

I will cling to the old rugged cross,
and exchange it someday for a crown.
—FROM "THE OLD RUGGED CROSS"
BY GEORGE BENNARD (1913)

George Bennard was a young evangelist and minister in 1912, traveling between cities to lead revivals in Michigan and Wisconsin. Though he was preaching and singing to rapt crowds during the revivals, privately he was struggling spiritually. He found himself studying John 3:16 and reflecting more and more on the image of the cross and the suffering of Christ. "I was going through a great travail," he explained many years later. "I needed help. Then I remembered an old wooden cross I had once seen. The first ten words came to me; 'On a hill far away stood an old rugged cross.'"[1] "The Old Rugged Cross" went on to become one of the most beloved hymns in American history.

When we, like Bennard, go thorough pain and suffering, we can look to the cross—the "emblem of suffering and shame"— and know that our Savior suffers with us and for us. He endured that terrible cross, giving us resurrection and life in exchange!

DAY 8

The Mixing Bowl

*When he had given thanks, he broke it,
and said, "This is my body, which is for
you; do this in remembrance of me."*
—1 CORINTHIANS 11:24

There is an olive green, porcelain mixing bowl in my kitchen that stirs up more than cake batter; it stirs up memories. My grandmother, Ruby, used that mixing bowl to whip up numerous Easter dishes. The bowl was passed down to my mom, who also used it to make many a holiday dessert. It now resides in my kitchen. I'll soon use it to make my daughter (named Ruby after her great-grandmother) an Easter treat, and with each stir of the batter, I'll remember Grandma Ruby.

What kinds of things remind you of your loved ones? You could probably begin listing several of them without much thought. Is there an old saying your dad always used? Or perhaps a certain recipe always makes you think of your mother. Do fresh tulips remind you of your sister? Memories are so powerful that they can make it seem as if the people who gave us those

memories are right there with us, even if they're far away. It is good to remember the ones we love.

As Jesus prepared for the cross, He wanted to give the apostles a way to remember Him. Yet He also wanted them to have more than just an assortment of memories or keepsakes. Yes, the healings were meaningful and His teachings were critical, but it was vital that His followers have a special ritual to remember the sacrifice He was about to make. After all, without that sacrifice and without His resurrection, everything Christ had done would have amounted to nothing more than great acts of kindness.

So Jesus gave them—and us—a way to remember. He gave them the Lord's Supper: the breaking of bread and the drinking from the cup. After that, every time the people gathered to break bread, they would recall His body on the cross and the way He emptied Himself on their behalf. The bread and the wine would always be a visual reminder of all He had given.

This Easter, take the time to remember Christ on the cross. Don't be afraid to think on His sorrow, His groaning and anguish. Because they were His gift to us. To save us. To save you. It's important to never forget the cost of salvation. Let's live our lives in remembrance of Jesus, living as He lived.

Thank You, Lord, for the *sacrifice* You made. Help me remember the price You *paid* for Your people, and the victory it has bought me.

DAY 9

One Goblet

After the supper he took the cup, saying, "This cup is the new covenant in my blood, which is poured out for you."
—LUKE 22:20

Have you ever felt as if your sin was more grievous than someone else's? Maybe the shame of what you've done or who you've been seems beyond redemption. Or, on the flip side, have you ever thought to yourself, *At least I haven't done* that . . . ? We like to compare, don't we? It's easy to view everything about ourselves in relation to someone else and then to determine how well we do—or don't—measure up. Why do we do that?

Some friends and I recently attended a church event in which communion was being offered. Now, there are several ways in which the Lord's Supper can be taken. Some churches will pass the elements on plates, and each Christ-follower can take a wafer and a cup of juice and pass the plate. Other churches may have stations set up for people to go and pick up the elements and then take them back to their seats.

This particular evening, there were two people standing at the front of the room. One held a plate and one held a goblet. Perhaps this is the norm for you, but this was new territory for me! My gaze was fixed on that one goblet, and I was desperately trying to determine how exactly this was all going to proceed. Was it full of tiny, individual servings of juice? I knew *that* was highly unlikely. Were we all really going to drink from the same cup? If so, I needed to wipe off my lipstick because I can't think of anything more embarrassing than leaving a lip print on the communion cup.

The introvert in me wanted to simply stay in my seat and pretend to be preoccupied with my phone. But then the self-conscious part of me thought, *People will think I don't love Jesus.* So I slowly stood and got in line. Mesmerized, I watched as each person walked to the front of the room, took a piece of bread from the plate, and dipped it into the goblet.

It was such a beautiful picture of the blood of Christ. Each person carried different burdens. Each held different hurts and needs. Yet the same blood—the same cup—cleansed each one. Christ's shed blood was for each and every person. No matter the sin, His blood was enough.

The Old Testament is filled with accounts of various blood offerings needed to atone for the different sins of the people. So much blood was needed to make a person only *temporarily* clean before God. But then Jesus came. He was the perfect lamb—the perfect sacrifice—who cleansed us once and for all and made a way for us to be right before the Father.

The next time you're tempted to compare your sins to another's, to declare yourself *worse* or *better*, take a step back and remember that all sins separate us from God, and there is nothing that Jesus' sacrifice does not cover. All are equal in His eyes. So put aside the comparisons, the pride, shame, and anything else that may hold you back. Jesus' blood covers it all.

DAY 10

Last Year's Easter Egg

*"While I was with them, I protected them and
kept them safe by that name you gave me.
None has been lost except the one doomed to
destruction so that Scripture would be fulfilled."*
—John 17:12

What is the most valuable thing you have ever lost? Does the thought of it still "stick in your craw," as my dad would say? We are just a losing-things kind of people. We leave purses in dressing rooms, cell phones at restaurants, and books on airplanes. Just the other day, I saw a woman driving around Bowling Green, Kentucky, with her coffee cup on the top of her car! Bet she was wondering where that went . . .

If you've ever run over an Easter egg with your lawn mower in May, you totally understand the saying "It's as lost as last year's Easter egg." There always seems to be one that was hidden just a little too well. How does that happen? Oddly enough, it's the same way we get lost in life ourselves.

First, we take on too much, and things fall through the cracks.

Sometimes we get a little too ambitious and hide more eggs than our little ones can ever hope to find. Have you ever found yourself biting off more than you can chew? Saying yes when everything in you wanted to say no? Making a home or work project just a little more complicated than it had to be? We have all been in that boat, my friend. Not only do we lose the things that fall through the cracks, but we also lose our sense of purpose and focus when we're overwhelmed.

Second, we tend to quit when things get difficult or even just boring. Have you ever tried to convince a three-year-old to keep looking for eggs long after the fun is over? Sure, they were all excited about hunting eggs when those eggs were sitting in plain sight on the mailbox. But we lose their interest with the ones hidden under the back porch. There comes a point in every little one's life when a plastic egg is no longer worth the effort. And there comes a time in our lives when we're so tired that we look around and think, *Why keep trying?*

If you feel as lost as last year's Easter egg, know that Someone has come to find you. Read today's verse again. Often called the "High Priestly Prayer," the words in John 17:1–26 may just be the most passionate prayer in all of Scripture. It was Jesus' prayer to

the Father, immediately preceding His betrayal and arrest. And do you know who was on the heart and mind of Jesus as He made His way to the cross? It was you and me. As His days on earth were drawing to an end, the Son prayed to the Father for those of us who would be trying to navigate this broken world below. Can you imagine the love and tenderness in His voice when He uttered, "None has been lost"?

Here is what we can know about our Savior: He has never taken on more than He could handle. We are not too much for Him. Our baggage is not too heavy. Our biggest problem never stumps Him. He isn't bored when we bring the same worry to Him over and over. Our needs are not too draining. Our worries are not too overwhelming. Jesus knew all that we would be and all that we would do, and He still deemed us worthy of His death. When Jesus looked up to the Father and said, "None has been lost," He meant us. He meant you.

DAY 11

An Easter Nap

*When he rose from prayer and went
back to the disciples, he found them
asleep, exhausted from sorrow.*
—LUKE 22:45

What is your go-to response when life is overwhelming? My automatic reflex to stress is a nap. There is something about going to sleep that shuts out the world for just a little while. Whether it's just the everyday stresses of life, financial struggles, or issues with loved ones, it's tempting just to pull the covers over our heads and disappear for a moment.

I believe that's what happened to the disciples in the Garden of Gethsemane. In Luke 22, Jesus asked His disciples to wait for Him while He went to pray. But when He returned, He found them sleeping. Now, be honest: have you ever kind of rolled your eyes in disgust and thought the disciples to be lazy men, or even heartless and uncaring? If so, it would be helpful to go back and read today's Scripture slowly and out loud.

Luke 22:45 tells us why the men were sleeping. They were

"exhausted from sorrow." Jesus had told them what was coming. The time was near, and they were consumed by sorrow and sadness. Now can you relate? Doesn't that make you see these men in a completely different and much more compassionate light?

When Jesus returned to find the men asleep, His response was, "Get up and pray *so that you will not fall into temptation*" (v. 46, emphasis added).

Satan is always waiting for an opportune time to strike (Luke 4:13). What better time to strike than when we are neglecting prayer, feeling overwhelmed, or retreating into isolation? Naps are good. Rest is necessary. Don't get me wrong—I am all about a restorative Sunday afternoon nap. But if sleep or escape is our go-to defense mechanism, we may want to rethink our pattern of behavior and refocus on our Father, who is big enough to handle any situation.

What if instead of sleeping or seeking physical comfort, our first instinct was to pray? We could ask Him to give us the energy just to do the next thing—to give us wisdom to know when to rest and when to carry on and seek His face in prayer through the night. The next time life seems a bit too much and you're tempted to hide, get up and pray instead.

DAY 12

Coloring Eggs

*After a little while, those standing there went
up to Peter and said, "Surely you are one
of them; your accent gives you away."*
—MATTHEW 26:73

Several years ago, I stayed up after the kids went to bed and dyed some Easter eggs to put in their baskets the next morning. It seemed like a fun idea, and the next morning I even went so far as to hint that the Easter bunny had been the one to deliver the goodies. While the other girls were going through the baskets and enjoying the candy, my second child came over to me.

"I know it was you," Ella whispered, giggling. "Your hands give you away."

Sure enough, though I had tried to wash it away, my fingers were lightly stained from the dye. I had tried to deny it, but my hands gave me away.

What is it about you that "gives you away" as a follower of Christ? Would it be the gentleness of your spirit or the way you love others? What is it that, when others see it, lets them know that you are "one of them"?

When Jesus was arrested, all the disciples fled. Scripture says that although Peter did follow the crowds as they led Jesus away, he did so at a distance. Peter wanted to see what was going on, but he was afraid to be associated with Christ at that point. And, just as Jesus had predicted, Peter denied knowing Him three times.

The crowd knew that Jesus' followers were from Galilee, and they had recognizable accents. So no matter how much Peter denied it, his accent gave him away.

Obviously, we don't ever want to deny Christ. But, like Peter, there should be something about us that makes it clear to those around us where our devotion lies. Early on in Jesus' earthly ministry, He taught the disciples an important lesson: a healthy tree bears good fruit while a diseased tree bears bad fruit (Matthew 7:17). A person can know whether a tree is healthy or not by the fruit it bears. The fruit gives it away every time.

Likewise, our fruit as a believer should give us away. We are told that the fruit of the Spirit is love, joy, peace, patience, kindness, goodness, faithfulness, gentleness, and self-control. May these things be so ingrained in you that those around you would say, "Surely you are one of them."

Help me live in such a way, Lord,

that *everything* about me

gives me away as one of Yours.

DAY 13

The Easter Lily

*Then Pilate announced to the chief
priests and the crowd, "I find no
basis for a charge against this man."*
—LUKE 23:4

Have you ever smelled the sweet fragrance of an Easter lily? Their white blossoms can fill the room with a heavy, intoxicating perfume. More than just a sweet smell and a pretty blossom, the lily is actually an amazing plant. You see, it doesn't grow in carefully cared-for and well-manicured flower beds. Its roots are not found in freshly tilled, sunbathed soil. No, the lily, one of the loveliest flowers to be found, grows in the mud. Its fragile beauty thrives amid the muck and mire surrounding lakes and streams. Many of us will have lilies in our homes for Easter. When you look upon their blooms, remember they are more than pretty flowers: they are survivors.

The lily's strong, pure white flower emerges out of the ooze and unpleasantness of the lake beds and riverbanks. No wonder it has come to represent the beauty of Easter. You see, Christ left

the beauty of heaven to live and love amid the muck and mire of earth. He touched the untouchable. He served the sinners. He taught tax collectors. He dined with disciples who would abandon Him, and He did not look away from those whom He knew would betray Him. He had compassion on the crowds. He loved the leper. He healed the hurting. And He did it all in a world that constantly warred against Him.

Christ walked the sin-stained soil of this earth yet remained perfectly pure. He was tempted in every way but was without sin. When Jesus was thrust before Pilate, the crowds were adamant that He was a danger to society. Scripture says they were "urgent" in their accusations (Luke 23:5 ESV). Yet when Pilate spoke with Jesus and surveyed the situation, he could find no guilt in Him. Jesus was innocent, pure, and unspoiled by the sin around Him. That's why we are able to trust Him. He endured the same sinful world that we now endure, dealt with the same temptations, and felt the same pain. Jesus knew what it was like to lose loved ones. He had tasted the sting of fickle friends. Yes, Christ was very well acquainted with the muck and mire, and yet He still emerged as the perfect Savior.

Let us not forget that the road to the cross was long. There

were many hardships and heartaches along the way. It wasn't an easy journey. The path was not well paved, free of all storms, or lined with tulips. But just as the lily is all the more beautiful because of the mud from which it comes, Christ is all the more beautiful because of what He endured for us.

Have you ever looked at your past and been fully aware that it was only the grace of God that brought you to where you are today? It's difficult to see the hope on the horizon when we are covered in the mud of the here and now. Only in looking back can we see how far He has brought us. God has a way of lifting us out of the muck and mire (Psalm 40:2).

DAY 14

Easter Bonnets

The soldiers twisted together a crown of thorns and put it on his head and arrayed him in a purple robe.

—John 19:2 ESV

What kind of hat looks best on you? Whether it's a baseball cap, a cowboy hat, or an Easter bonnet, hats make a statement. In my case, the statement is usually, "I didn't have time to fix my hair this morning, so I'm wearing a hat." That's probably not the look that the hatmaker intended!

The Easter bonnet, in particular, became popular in America in the 1930s when Irving Berlin penned the words, "I could write a sonnet about your Easter bonnet." Suddenly, women everywhere were looking for the perfect hat to complete their Easter ensembles. Many now-grown girls have memories of bonnets with strings that tied under their chins or with roses pinned to the side. The bonnet was the "finishing touch" added to the outfit before heading off to church.

But a hat can be so much more than decoration. It can be symbolic of a vocation, or—as in the case of our Savior—a

symbol of mockery. After Jesus was arrested and flogged, the soldiers cruelly decided He needed something more. They wanted to add something that would make a statement, a "finishing touch." So they made a crown of thorns and placed it on His head. It was meant to hurt and humiliate. It was intended to mock His claims of royalty and send a clear message to His followers. It was a case of adding insult to injury.

We know the soldiers laughed as they mockingly knelt before Him. But what did the followers of Jesus feel? Were they embarrassed? Did they realize that He was doing it all for them and for those who had not yet but would someday believe?

Regardless of the soldiers' intentions, the crown of thorns serves to remind us that Jesus is, in fact, the King. We know that He is now seated on His throne. Those who knelt to mock Him will one day kneel again and confess Him as Lord of all. Any "crowns" of glory that we may earn will be cast down at His feet when we reach heaven.

It's so important to remember that at any point on that journey to the cross, Jesus could have said, "Enough." But He didn't. He looked at all that He would have to endure and He deemed us worth it. Christ our King wore the crown of thorns for us.

I cannot fully *comprehend* the magnitude of Your sacrifice, Lord. But I thank You for *loving* me and considering me worth it.

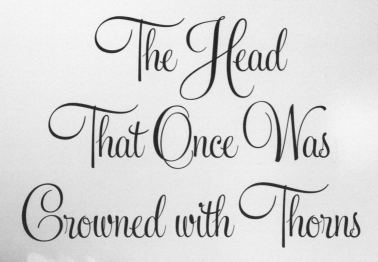

DAY 15

The Head
That Once Was
Crowned with Thorns

The head that once was crowned with thorns is crowned with glory now: a royal diadem adorns the mighty Victor's brow.
—from "The Head That Once Was Crowned with Thorns" by Thomas Kelly (1820)

At Easter time, in the midst of new beauty, we're faced with the jarring harshness of crucifixion symbols. The crown of thorns. The nails. The bloody cross. Instruments of death stand out starkly against the pastel background of the season. One might even think they seem out of place. Yet they are the whole reason for the celebration! This hymn reminds us that the ugly crown is a royal diadem now, that all these dark symbols mean something entirely different because of His victory.

So, tempted as we may be to upstage the not-so-pleasant aspects of Easter symbolism with doilies, bunnies, or buttercream icing, let's remember what a miracle it is that the things meant to cause Christ pain are now turned on their heads through His power and made beautiful for us. "Jesus [is] now crowned with glory and honor because he suffered death, so that by the grace of God he might taste death for everyone" (Hebrews 2:9).

DAY 16

A Walk of Remembrance

Then they led him out to crucify him.
—MARK 15:20

Are you one of those people who can't get by without a daily walk? In the morning with the birds or in the evening with the lightning bugs, with a faithful pet or in sweet solitude, a walk in the fresh air of God's creation can completely reset your mind. It can relax you, energize you, and give you perspective you didn't have before. It can remind you that people were made to visit with God during a walk "in the garden in the cool of the day" (Genesis 3:8). Perhaps that's why some church traditions practice "the way of the cross"—a contemplative walk designed to immerse us in Christ's walk toward His crucifixion.

Also called the Stations of the Cross or *Via Dolorosa* ("the way of sorrows"), this tradition involves fourteen stations set around a church or beautiful outdoor setting. As you walk in silence, you observe paintings at each station depicting an event in the passion of Christ. The journey begins at the Garden of Gethsemane, continuing with Jesus' betrayal, trial, beating, and

walk toward Golgotha, with His encounters along the way. At each station, walkers stop and remember. They pray and mourn. They thank and marvel, up until the final station—when He is laid in the tomb from which He will rise. The walk helps them remember, as God opens up their hearts to understand what His Son did for them.

This Easter season, take some time to walk the Stations of the Cross, whether at a local church or on a walk of your own. Carry with you the verses associated with each event. Pause and pray, remembering as you go. And with every step, ask God to show you anew what Christ accomplished on His walk of sorrows.

Jesus, I am so *grateful* that You walked toward death for me. Open my heart to further *understand* the sacrifice You made.

DAY 17

Picked Out of the Crowd

*As they were going out, they met a man
from Cyrene, named Simon, and they
forced him to carry the cross.*

—MATTHEW 27:32

When you were a child, did you ever get roped into the post-meal kitchen cleanup? You could always tell that it was about that time because the adults would start pushing plates back and the conversation would begin winding down. This is when you wanted to make yourself scarce, or you'd be elbow deep in dishwater before you knew it!

On the way to the cross, a man named Simon discovered a thing or two about being roped into something he didn't want to do. We don't know much about Simon of Cyrene. Scripture says he had just come in from the country, and he was in the crowd when Jesus was being led to His death. He was close enough to the action that, when the guards reached for someone, they were able to grab him. Before he knew it, he was carrying the cross and following in Jesus' footsteps.

When we decide to follow Jesus, we have no way of knowing what it will look like for us. We may simply serve Him behind the scenes. Yet we must also be prepared to be picked out of the crowd. We may be picked out for public ministry or put on the spot when sharing our faith. Matthias was the disciple chosen to replace Judas as one of the Twelve. One of the requirements for Judas's replacement was that he be someone who had been among the group from the beginning. It had to be someone who had accompanied the apostles during all the time when Jesus went in and out among them (Acts 1:21). Just like that, someone who had faithfully followed was given a new assignment.

Other times, we will be picked out for acts of sacrifice in the name of Jesus. Simon had no way of knowing that he would end up with a cross on his back. But are we ever closer to Jesus than when we feel the weight of the cross?

Whether you are to be Matthias or Simon, always be prepared to be picked. How? By being faithful in the study of God's Word. By being consistent in prayer. By being prepared with a heart of trust, willing to go wherever God calls you—even when it's unexpected.

Lord, help me always be *prepared* to be used by You. May I be ready to serve and *sacrifice* when You call my name.

I Have Decided to Follow Jesus

*I have decided to follow Jesus; I have decided
to follow Jesus; I have decided to follow
Jesus; no turning back, no turning back.*
—from "I Have Decided to Follow
Jesus," Author Unknown

Simon of Cyrene didn't get to choose whether to follow Jesus that day when Pilate's soldiers seized him and made him carry Jesus' cross. Yet it's easy to imagine that the incident left an indelible mark on his life and his family for generations. How could it not? Some scholars suggest that his son Rufus was the one the apostle Paul referred to as "chosen in the Lord," a worker in the early church in Rome (Romans 16:13). If it's true, Simon's involuntary encounter sparked a faith that helped spread Jesus' message throughout the world in the early days of Christianity.

Today we get to decide to follow Jesus too—no turning back—and pass down the stories of our encounters with Jesus to generations to follow. Whatever's behind us, we take up our cross daily and follow Him (Luke 9:23). Even if none go with us, we tell those around us. Until we see Jesus.

DAY 19

*That's
My King*

Above his head they placed the written charge against him: THIS IS JESUS, THE KING OF THE JEWS.
—MATTHEW 27:37

*H*ow are you at describing things? Can you wax poetic, or do you fumble for the right words? Just the other day, on a popular television show, a couple was asked to list three things that they loved about their spouse. The husband was instantly able to share three things, and his words were heartfelt and romantic. The poor wife, on the other hand, was painful to watch. She played with her ring and sat there as the seconds ticked away. Either from nerves or from lack of inspiration, she could not verbalize one thing that she loved about her husband!

S. M. Lockridge was a pastor for more than forty years, and he had no problem describing his love for the Lord. Though he pastored a church in California, he is most known for a sermon he delivered in Detroit in 1976. Millions of people have listened to this sermon over the years, and it continues to captivate the hearts of listeners. The sermon, *That's My King*, is a

six-and-a-half-minute description of Jesus. Trust me: you want to look it up and listen to it. Just know beforehand that you will want to jump out of your chair or, at the very least, shout, "Amen!"

A few of Lockridge's descriptors for Jesus are:

He's enduringly strong.
He's entirely sincere.
He's eternally steadfast.
He's the doorway of deliverance.
He's the pathway to peace.
He's the gateway of glory.[1]

If we call ourselves Christ-followers, we are to always be prepared to give a reason for the hope that we have (1 Peter 3:15). If someone asked us to list three things we love about Jesus, the words should just tumble right out of us. Each of us should have a heart so overflowing with love for Him that we'd be able to write our own "That's My King" sermon.

What is there to love about Jesus? He takes our rubble and rebuilds us. He takes our brokenness and makes it beautiful. He takes our jagged pieces and gives us His peace. He calls us

by name and removes our shame. The more we see of Him, the more we *want* to see of Him.

Our Lord lay in a manger, hung on a cross, and walked out of a tomb. He taught and touched. He healed and loved. No one was invisible in His presence or beyond the reach of His power. Jesus, my friend, is everything. He is more than enough for whatever you face.

There is more to Jesus than we could ever comprehend. Make it your prayer that He would reveal more and more of Himself to you each day. Though His persecutors named Him "King of the Jews," He is King of so much more—so much that mere words are not enough to describe Him. May we have an unquenchable thirst to know our King more and more each day!

DAY 20

The Choice

They crucified two rebels with him,
one on his right and one on his left.
—MARK 15:27

There is something you need to know about making corn-bread muffins. Once you mix the ingredients, you need to let the batter rest for about four minutes before spooning it into the muffin tin. This will maximize the crown on your muffin. And who, pray tell, does not want the best crown possible on their corn muffins?

Here's the thing, though. Now that you've been told this secret truth, you can't *un*know it. From here on out, if you make corn muffins, you will be forced to make a choice: maximum crowns or mediocre crowns.

And so it is with the knowledge of Christ. Every person who has ever come into contact with Christ has made a choice. It's impossible to be in His presence and not be affected.

The two thieves on the cross perfectly illustrate this Easter choice. Both men had been sentenced to death for the crimes

they had committed. Both were equally guilty in the eyes of the law. Neither of them was deserving of grace or mercy. And at the cross, both men were faced with the same choice: accept or reject Jesus.

One man chose to take the same mocking tone as the crowd. Scripture says that this criminal "railed" at Jesus (Luke 23:39 ESV). The Greek word is *blasphēmeō* and is often translated as "to blaspheme" or "to speak evil of."[1] This man made his choice.

The other criminal rebuked the first and spoke beseechingly to Christ. He begged to be remembered when Jesus entered His kingdom. The thief confessed his faith in Jesus and pleaded for His mercy. This man, also, made his choice.

At some point, each of us faces that same Easter choice. We can never say that we didn't know, for all of creation points to the Creator (Romans 1:20). We cannot claim to have not heard. And we can't pretend that we haven't seen.

Take time this Easter season to choose and *re*-choose Jesus each day, being humble enough to acknowledge your brokenness and bold enough to ask Jesus to make you whole.

I *choose* You, Lord.

I choose You as *Savior* and Lord.

DAY 21

Around the Table

*Near the cross of Jesus stood his mother,
his mother's sister, Mary the wife of
Clopas, and Mary Magdalene.*

—John 19:25

What are some of your favorite Easter memories? For most of us, the details we remember most are the ones that revolve around the people we were with. Perhaps you recall the cousins all gathering to color eggs. Maybe everyone tended to gather at a certain person's house. You probably still remember who brought the deviled eggs and who would fall asleep in that old plaid recliner. It's the people who make the memories. The ones who gather around your table matter.

As I remember Easters past, I can name every person who gathered around our table. I can call them by their given names and even their nicknames. There was Gertrude, but everyone called her Gertie. Wilbert Sr. went by Woody, while Wilbert Jr. was Butch. Faces and names are etched in my memory because they are *my* people. You, no doubt, have your own memories and could recite the names of *your* people.

Many times in Scripture, individuals are not specifically named for us. For example, we don't know the names of the thieves who hung on the crosses by Jesus at Golgotha, or the names of the soldiers who tortured Him. We can only assume that we weren't given their names because, in those instances, it wasn't critical that we know.

But some names are important, such as those that John listed by name in his gospel. They were important and they were included because they were Jesus' people. They were the ones who had walked with Him, talked with Him, and lived life with Him—Mary, His mother; Mary Magdalene; and John, the beloved disciple. These were Jesus' people, and they stood watch there with Him, at the foot of the cross.

This Easter season, pay careful attention to the people who surround you—who are closest to you. Look them in the eye and call them by name. The ones who choose to do life with you matter. There will be a time when you'll look back and recall the very moment you're in right now. It won't matter that the Enemy mocked, and you won't bother remembering those who were just passing by. But you'll smile fondly when you speak the names of those who loved you—your people.

I am so *grateful*, Lord, that when You look upon humanity, You don't see a mass of people. You see *individuals*, and You know each of us by name—even me.

DAY 22

A Taste of Vinegar

A jar of wine vinegar was there, so they soaked a sponge in it, put the sponge on a stalk of the hyssop plant, and lifted it to Jesus' lips.

—JOHN 19:29

Are there any holiday traditions that you just assumed everyone does? Maybe you thought everyone had sauerkraut for New Year's Eve. As a Northerner who married a Southerner, I'll let you in on a little secret. Not everyone does sauerkraut. Apparently, black-eyed peas are a thing too.

At Easter, one dish that was always on our table was pickled eggs. (If you just curled your nose, it's okay. We can still be friends.) They're just hard-boiled eggs placed in a jar with oil, vinegar, and beets and left to soak up the flavor. As it turns out, there's a long history of pickling foods for Easter. In many areas, it's common to pickle fish. (There really isn't much more to say about that. It's fish. And it's pickled.)

It can be rewarding to learn why we have certain traditions. By taking the time to fully grasp each element of this season,

we can stop ourselves from treating it like any other day on the calendar. For instance, using vinegar to pickle foods during this season is reminiscent of the vinegar offered to Jesus on the cross. Though it may seem like only a small detail, we don't want to gloss over it. Since it was important enough to be included in Scripture, it's something we should remember and ponder.

At this point in the crucifixion narrative, Jesus was very close to breathing His last breath. He had cried out to the Father and, as the crowds continued to mock, He said, "I thirst." They offered Him vinegar on a sponge to quench His thirst. A minor detail, perhaps, but it is one more enlightening piece in the picture of His sacrifice.

Before Christ was actually on the cross, the gospel of Mark mentions the soldiers offering Him vinegar (15:23). It was common for those sentenced to death to be given a drug, mixed with wine vinegar, in order to dull the senses and lessen the pain. Jesus refused this first offering.

After He was on the cross and had suffered for some time, Jesus cried out to the Father. Bystanders thought He was calling out for Elijah to take Him off the cross (Mark 15:35). At this point, they offered Jesus the vinegar again, not to help Him, but

in the hope of keeping Him conscious longer and prolonging His pain.

David Mathis explains it this way: "Other condemned criminals would have taken the first (to ease their torment) and passed on the second (so as not to prolong their horrific pain). But Jesus would take no shortcuts on the way to our redemption."[1]

This Easter, as you gather around the table, take note of those foods that use vinegar. At our house, we'll have pickled eggs on the table. But this year, they will be more than a delicious side dish; they'll serve as a reminder of just how far Jesus was willing to go, and how much He was willing to suffer, so we could be at peace with the Father.

DAY 23

The Easter
Egg Hunt

Now there was a man named Joseph . . . and
he was looking for the kingdom of God.

—Luke 23:50–51 esv

*I*f you have ever taken a child on a first Easter egg hunt, you know that it can be fun and frustrating all at the same time. When my middle daughter, Sarah, was younger, she would do one of two things: she would either stand in the middle of the yard waiting for someone to drop eggs into her basket, or she would just follow one of her sisters around hoping to get a hand-out. I'll just tell you that neither of those things usually happened. It's every girl for herself in our family Easter egg hunts!

Sarah had to learn an important lesson: if something is important to you, you have to seek it for yourself.

The gospels record an important moment after Jesus' death, when we meet Joseph of Arimathea. Joseph was a good and upright man. He was a member of the council, so he would have been well known and respected. More importantly, Scripture says that Joseph was "looking for the kingdom of God." He didn't

agree with the decisions and actions of the Jewish leadership as they condemned Jesus. Could it be that, because he was looking, Joseph saw things they didn't see?

After the crucifixion, Joseph went to Pilate and asked for the body of Jesus. He personally "took down the body" of Christ from the cross (Mark 15:46). It is so tempting to rush through Scripture because we think we have heard it all before, but don't do that here. Imagine yourself in this moment. Joseph—a disciple of Christ, though secretly because he feared the Jews (John 19:38)—now stepping forward to tend to His Savior. In his efforts, he was helped by Nicodemus, who had also once visited Christ in the secrecy of night (John 3:1–21).

We don't know many of the details of this moment, but what we *do* know is that Joseph was allowed to physically see and touch what he had been seeking for so long. He made the effort, and his effort was rewarded—not only by the honor of tending to the body of Christ but also by His resurrection. Hebrews tells us that God is a rewarder of those who diligently seek Him (Hebrews 11:6). What better reward could there be than to see Jesus?

Seek Him, sweet friend. He is so worth the effort.

You are all things *beautiful*, Lord, and there is nothing on earth that *compares*. Keep my heart forever seeking You.

DAY 24

Your Most Precious Thing

Taking Jesus' body, the two of them
wrapped it, with the spices, in strips of linen.
—John 19:40

Do you have something in your house that's so fancy you never use it? A set of delicate dishes? Linen napkins that are no match for stains? What kind of guest would it take for you to pull out your most precious things and use them?

Jesus was that guest for Mary, Martha, and Lazarus. In the story in John 12, Martha served a special meal, and Lazarus sat with Him and talked. But Mary thought that wasn't enough. She took a rare jar of perfume, potentially the most expensive thing she had, and broke it over His feet. She didn't give Him a simple spritz, saving some for later. She didn't just share a bit of her best as a kind gesture. She broke it, beyond repair, and spread it on her Savior's feet with her own hair. That's beyond hospitality. That's worship.

When Judas criticized her for being so wasteful, Jesus told him, "Leave her alone. . . . It was intended that she should save

this perfume for the day of my burial" (John 12:7). *His burial.* All Jesus' talk of His death must have been hard for His disciples to hear. But maybe Mary looked at her brother—Lazarus, who was raised from the dead—and wondered if her Lord was not subject to death's finality. She gave her all in an exuberant act of worship—anointing for burial the One who defeated death.

Later, when Nicodemus and Joseph of Arimathea anointed Jesus' body with seventy-five more pounds of spices, the job was complete. He was buried according to custom, but He rose according to God's miraculous power, fulfilling prophecy and turning sorrow to unspeakable joy.

This season, when you think of Christ's burial, remember Mary and pour out your very best to Him with a grateful heart. Whether it's showing hospitality in His name, worshiping in spirit and truth, serving those who are hurting, or giving of your resources, don't hold back. He is more than worth it.

Thank You, Lord, for *defeating* death for me. Please accept my very best as I give to You without *reservation.*

DAY 25

Rolled Away

"Take a guard," Pilate answered. "Go, make the tomb as secure as you know how." So they went and made the tomb secure by putting a seal on the stone and posting the guard.

—MATTHEW 27:65–66

*H*ave you ever felt as if something were holding you back? Do you ever feel bound by fear, insecurity, or the need to please? Maybe, in your heart, you know that Christ has set you free, but you still are not currently living in freedom. You're not alone.

I read an article many years ago about elephants kept in captivity. Elephants are some of the largest animals in the world and weigh thousands of pounds. Yet these massive animals were often kept in place with simple ankle restraints. With only the smallest effort, an elephant could have broken those kinds of shackles. Why didn't they?

Because being shackled was all they had known. The individuals responsible for maintaining the animals began shackling

the elephants when they were just babies. At first, perhaps, the animals did attempt to break the chains, but at that point they were not strong enough. By the time they had the strength to fight for freedom, they were so used to the chains that they didn't even try. Can you imagine? All that stood between a massive elephant and freedom was the realization that it was stronger than the chains that bound it.

The disciples must have looked at the stone covering Jesus' tomb and felt the shackles click into place. That stone was surely immovable to them. They had been a part of Jesus' ministry from the beginning. They had heard His teachings and witnessed His healings.

They had left everything to follow Him. Yet not in their wildest imaginings could they have envisioned what would happen. The betrayal. The cross. The tomb. The rock rolled into place.

The betrayal was brutal. The cross was cruel. The tomb was cold. But it was the rock that seemed to mock everything they thought was true. That rock was intentionally placed there to ensure that Jesus' body would not be moved. There would be no coming back from the grave. *Well, that's that,* they must have thought. But that wasn't that! The story was far from over! While

the people on the outside of the tomb were busy focusing on the rock, God was at work inside the tomb. There was no rock in all of creation that could have held Jesus in that grave, because the One who made the rock was stronger—and He knew it!

We will all face obstacles in our lives that Satan would love for us to look at and think, *Well, that's that.* It could be some sort of loss. Or perhaps we've failed in some area and are suffering the consequences. It could be a dream that, for some reason, has not yet come to fruition. Whatever the particular situation, it can seem as if a rock has been rolled into place, sealing off any hope of peace, or healing, or freedom from the shackles that bind us.

But here is what we must remember: the God who rolled the rock away is the same God who can roll our shame and pain away. We don't have to be held back by the things of this world. Greater is He who is in us than he who is in the world (1 John 4:4)! Stop focusing on every rock the Enemy rolls into place. Choose, instead, to keep your eyes on the One who is willing and able to roll the rock away—and set you free.

DAY 26

Sunday's Comin'

"For as Jonah was three days and three nights in the belly of a huge fish, so the Son of Man will be three days and three nights in the heart of the earth."

—Matthew 12:40

Can you think of a time when the days went faster or slower than you would have liked? It's true that time does seem to fly when you're having fun. But we can all agree that the opposite is also most certainly true. Time can move slower than molasses if you're struggling. Have you ever found yourself in a situation that you thought would never end? Perhaps a long, cold winter or a prolonged illness? When you're hurting, three days can be an eternity.

Three days is also the duration of the first Thanksgiving. It's the equivalent of a long weekend, a short vacation, or a bad stomach bug. Jonah spent three days and three nights in the belly of a big old fish. A lot can happen in three days—for good or for bad.

For three days, Christ lay in the grave. But after three days, He broke the chains of sin and death. And because of those three days, the Enemy was forever defeated, and we need never feel nor

fear the sting of death. Such good news—after three days. But there is a huge difference between the beginning and the ending of those three days.

For those at the foot of the cross, Friday was dark. Scripture says that when the people saw what happened, they beat their breasts and went away. While we have the luxury of knowing what happened on Sunday, they could not see beyond Friday.

S. M. Lockridge described it well in his famous sermon excerpt, "It's Friday, But Sunday's Comin'." This is just a portion of that now famous piece.

> It's Friday. Hope is lost. Death has won. Sin has conquered.
> And Satan's just a laughin'. It's Friday. Jesus is buried. A soldier
> stands guard. And a rock is rolled into place. But it's Friday. It
> is only Friday. Sunday is a comin'![1]

The people thought Friday was the end, but it was only the beginning. There will be Fridays, dear friend. There will be dark days and sad times. We just need to remember that Sunday *is* coming. God is still at work. The story does not end here. Hold on until Resurrection Sunday.

The Fridays of *life* can be

so very dark, Lord. Thank You

for the gift of *Sunday.*

DAY 27

The Looker

*As they were frightened and bowed their faces
to the ground, the men said to them, "Why
do you seek the living among the dead?"*
—LUKE 24:5 ESV

When you're searching for something, what kind of "looker" are you? There are basically three kinds. The first kind looks in logical places. This person looks around the yard and thinks, *If I were an Easter egg, where would I be?*

Then there's the "off-the-beaten-path" looker—and I mean *way* off. This is the person who begins looking for the Easter eggs in the neighbor's chicken coop or in the outside trash can. We all know this person. Some of us *are* this person. It takes all kinds, my friend.

The third kind of looker is the one who begins looking in logical places, but at some point, out of sheer desperation, begins frantically looking anywhere and everywhere for the thing they seek. One minute, they're looking on low-hanging tree branches, and then suddenly they're peering into the lawn mower's exhaust pipe and contemplating all sorts of crazy places.

The women who went out in search of Jesus' body that Sunday after the crucifixion were logical lookers. They were looking for a dead man, so *logically* they went to His tomb. But what they found was the stone rolled away and Christ's body gone. They began to panic because they could not fathom where else Jesus' body could be. But the tomb wasn't the right place at all—because the Son of God was anything but dead. He had risen. He was—and is—*alive*.

When you set out to look for love or for purpose in your life, are you a logical looker or an off-the-beaten-path looker? Have you ever found yourself looking in all the wrong places? We all have a desire to matter and to be a part of something bigger than ourselves. It's a noble desire, but it is one that can never be fulfilled outside of Christ.

Regardless of where you've looked before, you can choose to begin looking to Christ to meet your every need. Be the kind of looker who knows where to search to find fulfillment for the void within. If you're sad, lonely, or broken, take it to Jesus. Stop looking at the empty tombs in your life and, instead, seek the risen Savior.

Forgive me, Lord, for *looking* to the world to satisfy me. My heart is prone to *wander*. Teach me to seek only You.

Open My Eyes, That I May See

Open my eyes, that I may see glimpses of truth thou hast for me. Place in my hands the wonderful key that shall unclasp and set me free.
—FROM "OPEN MY EYES, THAT I MAY SEE"
BY CLARA H. SCOTT (1895)

This old hymn reminds us that God doesn't leave us stumbling around in the dark when we're seeking Him. Take a moment to sing Clara H. Scott's classic work, and notice what she asks God: "Open my eyes. . . . Open my ears. . . . Open my mouth. . . . Open my heart."

Though sometimes it may feel like we've wandered too far and are looking in futile places, God reminds us that He equipped us with senses and tools that we can turn toward Him. He gave us our eyes; when we ask Him to open them, He leads us toward freedom. He gave us our ears; and while they might be bombarded with distracting noise from the world, when we ask Him to open them, He will whisper to us, "This is the way; walk in it" (Isaiah 30:21). And when we wait on Him in grateful anticipation, He will open our mouths and hearts, and joyful praise will spill out!

Sweet Friendship

When Jesus rose early on the first day of the week, he appeared first to Mary Magdalene.
—MARK 16:9

Strong, ongoing relationships positively influence our physical, mental, and emotional health. A 2009 *New York Times* article attested to the importance of friendship, citing a study done at the University of Virginia. Thirty-four students were taken to the bottom of a steep hill and given a heavy backpack to wear. They were then asked to estimate the steepness of the hill. Some of the students were allowed to have friends standing next to them, while others stood alone. Those individuals with friends by their side gave lower estimates of the hill's steepness. The hill seemed much steeper to those who faced it alone.[1]

Jesus and Mary Magdalene were friends. She was part of Jesus' inner circle, often mentioned along with the Twelve. While we don't know much about her backstory, we do know that she had been demon-possessed and that Jesus had set her free. While others may have received their healing and moved

on, Mary lingered. She chose to stay close and became a constant presence in Christ's life.

While others were afraid to be associated with Jesus, Mary was there as He made His way through the towns, teaching and healing (Luke 8:1–2). When others betrayed Him and turned away, Mary stood by the cross as Jesus suffered (Matthew 27:56). Others returned to their homes after Jesus' death, but Mary was an eyewitness to Jesus' burial (Mark 15:47). And when His body was gone, she begged the man she thought to be the gardener to tell her where Jesus' body had been taken. Why? Because she was willing to go and get it back (John 20:15)! And, because of her absolute devotion to Christ, she was in a position to be the first to see Him risen from the grave (Mark 16:9)!

That is devotion.

Let's be that kind of friend. We can be the ones who stay when others walk away. We can be present in the midst of people's joy and pain. And then, we can be the ones to witness God raising them from the ashes and using it all for His glory.

Lord, You teach me so much by the way that You *lived*. Help me to be like You and Mary Magdalene and to *love* others well.

DAY 30

The Chrysalis

Peter, however, got up and ran to the tomb.
Bending over, he saw the strips of linen
lying by themselves, and he went away,
wondering to himself what had happened.

—LUKE 24:12

One of my favorite things about spring is the appearance of butterflies. Each year, my children and I purchase a butterfly garden and some caterpillars. We feed them, love them, and, of course, name them. Time passes, and each caterpillar attaches itself to the top of the container, shrouding itself in a chrysalis. It is all very mysterious to the children, and I hear the same questions every year: *What is happening? Are they dead?*

There is some confusion and a little bit of fear. After all, they have grown to love these caterpillars. Several times a day, the children will rush to the garden to see if anything has changed. And then it happens! One child will notice a change, and then another and another, until one day, they peek into the garden to see empty chrysalis shells and little butterflies fluttering about. Oh, the excitement of this discovery!

When Mary Magdalene and the other women found the tomb empty and were told that Jesus had risen, they hurried to tell the apostles. While some didn't believe, Peter immediately rose and ran to the tomb. He bent over, looked in, and saw them—the strips of linen that had once bound the body of Jesus were lying by themselves. Jesus had emerged from the grave and left His grave clothes behind. He no longer needed them!

Nothing about Jesus' life, death, or resurrection was an accident. He could have very easily risen in the grave clothes. He could have allowed Himself to be seen wrapped in linen. But Christ wanted to make it clear that no part of the grave still had a hold on Him. The linen strips lying there were vivid reminders that He had, in fact, been dead. And in leaving them behind, Jesus was making it clear that He was, and is, truly alive.

We all face dark times, when we feel confused or fearful. We endure the loss of things we've grown to love. We think, *What is happening? What is God doing?* Yet in God's infinite wisdom and goodness, sometimes He removes things from our lives that we thought we needed. In those moments, take another look. The old wrappings point to the soaring freedom of an eternal future in Christ. There is a message of life in the linens left behind.

Lord, please put my dark times in *perspective*. Keep me mindful of all that You left behind in order to bring me *forward* into new life.

DAY 31

Christ the Lord
Is Risen Today!

Christ the Lord is risen today, Alleluia!
Earth and heaven in chorus say, Alleluia!
Raise your joys and triumphs high, Alleluia!
Sing, ye heavens, and earth reply, Alleluia!
—FROM "CHRIST THE LORD IS RISEN TODAY!"
BY CHARLES WESLEY (1739)

When you hear this hymn, does that distinctive "Alleluia!" stick in your head all day long? It's such a triumphant sound! But did you know that Charles Wesley, one of the greatest hymn writers of all time, didn't originally include that *alleluia* in the text to this song? It was added later by a hymnbook editor, along with its rousing tune. Yet it is the perfect addition to Wesley's victorious lyrics.

All throughout Lent we've reflected on Christ's sacrifice, His love for us, and His atoning mercy. Some faith traditions even remove the word *alleluia* from liturgical texts during Lent so they can focus on repentance and reflect on the kingdom to come.[1] But on Easter it returns triumphantly! Christ the Lord *is* risen, and *now* we soar where He has led. So as you celebrate the victorious Christ, see what difference an added *alleluia* can make in your words and in your thoughts.

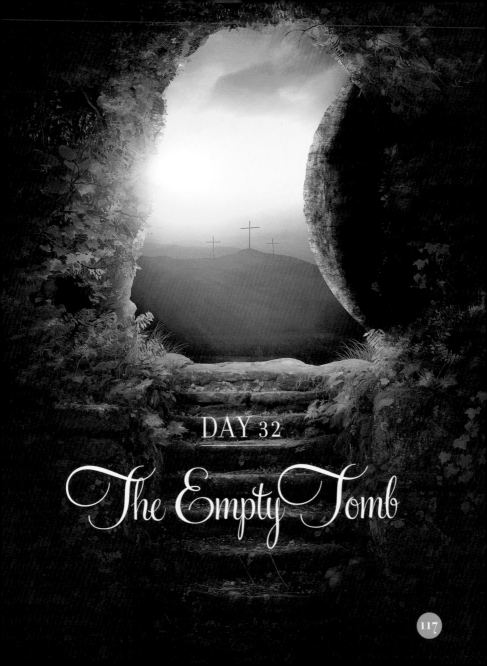

DAY 32

The Empty Tomb

"Don't be alarmed," he said. "You are looking for
Jesus the Nazarene, who was crucified. He has risen!
He is not here. See the place where they laid him."
—MARK 16:6

What is your favorite Easter tradition? At our house, we like to whip up a batch of resurrection rolls. Have you heard of them? If not, don't worry; I'm going to tell you all you need to know. To begin, you'll need a tube of crescent roll dough, large marshmallows, butter, and cinnamon sugar. (How can these be bad?) Then you start the assembly process. Are you ready? This is how they work.

Separate each crescent roll into individual triangles; each one will represent a tomb. Dip a large marshmallow (representing the body of Christ) in melted butter, and roll it in the cinnamon and sugar mixture (representing the preparation of the body before burial). Place the marshmallow on the crescent roll triangle and wrap the dough tightly around it (in other words, seal the tomb). Bake the rolls according to the package's instructions.

Now here is my challenge to you: Do not walk away. Don't use that time to check social media or take care of household tasks. Be still. Let the seconds tick away. Contemplate the gravity of the tomb. Imagine what it would have been like, knowing that the One you loved the most was behind the stone—and knowing that it was, most certainly, the One who loved *you* most.

When the resurrection rolls finish baking, remove them and let them cool. I'm sure you know what comes next. As you open the rolls, you will find that the marshmallow has melted and the "body of Christ" is gone. The tomb is empty! As Brother Glenn would say, "If that don't light your fire, your wood must be wet."

What happened inside that tomb is a marvelous mystery. Did angels hover? Was there a holy gasp from heaven when the stone was rolled into place? Was the Father counting each second that passed until it was time to whisper to His Son, "Rise and come home"?

The disciples had been told, both in parables and plain speech, that the resurrection would take place. Yet apparently they did not understand that He must rise from the dead (John 20:9.) It is tempting, with our modern luxuries of study Bibles and commentaries, to judge them. After all, they had walked

with Jesus as He healed and taught. They had heard Him talk about destroying and raising the temple. *How could they not understand?* But I ask, how *could* they have known the wonder of the Christ rising from the grave?

We may not know the secrets of the tomb, but there is something we do know: the Christmas manger was always about the cross, and the cross was always about the empty tomb. They are intricately linked, and all three events—birth, death, and resurrection—had to take place in order for us to be given the hope of salvation. When writing to the Corinthians, Paul said, "If Christ has not been raised, then our preaching is in vain and your faith is in vain" (1 Corinthians 15:14 ESV).

Christ is risen, sweet friend. He is risen, indeed.

DAY 33

Jelly Bean

Surprise

*Beginning with Moses and all the Prophets,
he explained to them what was said in all
the Scriptures concerning himself.*
—Luke 24:27

What is your favorite Easter candy? There are so many to choose from! The Easter candy of all candies, however, is the jelly bean. There are fifty official flavors of Jelly Belly jelly beans, and even more when you combine two flavors at once. All those choices can be slightly overwhelming. In fact, there are so many possible combinations that the Jelly Belly company publishes an actual flavor guide. If you have ever been faced with a bowl full of jelly beans in endless combinations and mysterious colors, you can appreciate how helpful such a guide would be to you.

If "life is like a bowl of jelly beans," God's Word serves as a guide to us in the choices we make. We can read it and study it. We can take it apart and look at it piece by piece. We can go back and forth and see how it all works together. God guides us through His Word, and He tells us which way to go.

When Jesus was crucified and buried, some of His followers were confused. They thought, perhaps, they had missed something or misunderstood. This wasn't the combination of events they were expecting!

Imagine the relief the two men on the road to Emmaus felt when Jesus reached out to them. His explanation started all the way back at the beginning to guide them through all that had happened. He didn't leave them on their own. He didn't make them fend for themselves and figure it out by trial and error. He gave them the guide.

We can attempt to navigate this life without utilizing the guide given to us. We can pop a jelly bean in our mouth and risk it being a chili mango one or accidentally combine popcorn and licorice (yuck!). Or, before taking a single step, we can turn to Scripture. We can ask the Lord to reveal Himself. Let's seek guidance from God's Word, and surround ourselves with those who do too.

DAY 34

"People Feet"

*But we had hoped that he was the
one who was going to redeem Israel.*
—LUKE 24:21

*D*isappointment. It showed up unexpectedly one Easter
when my daughter Emily got all dressed up to see the
Easter Bunny. Covered in lace and giddiness, she waited patiently
in line, and then it happened. The Easter Bunny knelt down on
one knee to hug the child in front of her—and Emily saw the
sole of a tennis shoe. The look on her face was one of horror as
she exclaimed to everyone around her, "The Easter Bunny has
people feet!" There is no way to make a gracious exit after that.

When was the last time you were disappointed? It's a
common scenario; we all have been let down by someone or
something. We buy things that don't live up to their advertised
promises. We put our faith in people who walk away. We accept
a job that turns out to be nothing like we'd anticipated. Life often
fails to live up to our expectations.

Many people following Jesus had built up some serious
expectations in terms of what "His kingdom" would look like.

They saw His miracles and heard His messages but misunderstood His mission. They were expecting royalty, and instead, they were presented with a man who sat with sinners and touched the untouchables. There was so much about Jesus that went against everything they thought they wanted.

Following Jesus' death, two men were walking down a road to their village, discussing all that had just taken place. They had hoped that this Jesus of Nazareth would be the One to rescue God's people and to restore Israel to her former glory. Imagine their *disappointment* as He was crucified! He was supposed to be the Messiah and, yet, He died! It seemed that their long-awaited Savior had "people feet," so to speak. What they had hoped for and what they actually got did not seem to be the same thing. It wasn't until Jesus opened their eyes (Luke 24:31) that they were able to see the situation for all that it truly was.

Life will offer you many disappointments. There will be many scenarios which will leave you uttering the words, "But I had hoped . . ." In those times, remember that you don't see everything clearly. But one day, thanks to His sacrifice, you'll be in His presence and see Him as He truly is. On that day, there will be absolutely no disappointment.

Lord, thank You for *leaving* Your throne above and taking on flesh for me. *Teach* me to trust You with my heart when I do not *understand* what my eyes see.

DAY 35

The Gathering Place

On the evening of that day, the first day of the week,
the doors being locked where the disciples were
for fear of the Jews, Jesus came and stood among
them and said to them, "Peace be with you."
—JOHN 20:19 ESV

My Aunt Nona's house was a special gathering place for our family. She had a lovely screened-in front porch, but as they say in the South, front doors are for strangers. Friends and family knew to walk around back and come on in. You didn't have to knock at Aunt Nona's place. You just opened the screen door and walked into a kitchen full of laughter and the smell of coffee. The kitchen was where everyone gathered.

The gathering place for Jesus and the apostles was the Upper Room. While its exact location is not known, we do know that these men met in this room when they stayed in Jerusalem. It was their place to meet, to fellowship, and just to be with Jesus. Can you even imagine the conversations that must have happened there?

It made perfect sense, then, that this was the place the

resurrected Christ chose to appear to them as a group—in this place where they could look around and know where each person sat, where they could still envision Christ kneeling to wash their feet. Yes, this would be the place the apostles would return to when their world seemed to be shattered.

Scripture tells us that the apostles had locked themselves in the Upper Room because they feared the Jews. And though the door was locked, Jesus came right on in—because this was where His people were gathered. You don't have to knock at a place like that. Jesus knew where His people would be, and He knew they would be afraid. "Peace be with you," Jesus said. How His voice must have soothed their souls!

In what place do you find yourself today? Is it a place of comfort, or has life gotten a little crazy? Do you find yourself wondering what to do next? Life gets that way for all of us at times. The good news is we don't have to frantically search for Jesus. He's looking for us, and there's not a locked door in this world that can keep Him from coming in. Choose to be still in the midst of the chaos; let Him find you. Know that Jesus will come to the Upper Room of your heart and be present in both your joy and your pain. And He will fill you with peace.

I am so *grateful*, Lord, that You know right where to *find* me. You know what I need, and You are *always* enough.

DAY 36

The Easter Ham

*And with that he breathed on them
and said, "Receive the Holy Spirit."*

—JOHN 20:22

*I*s there a meal or a certain dish that you prepare just the way your mama or your grandma did? Something that just wouldn't taste right to you if even the slightest ingredient were changed? We do what we know, right?

There is a story that has been passed around for years about a new bride who was cooking an Easter ham for her new husband. The husband noticed that before she put the ham in the baking dish, she cut off a small slice from each side and threw it in the trash. When he questioned her, the bride simply stated, "That's how mama always did it." It's hard to argue with that.

Sometime later, the bride's mama came to visit, and they happened to be having ham. "Why is it," the husband asked, "that you cut the ends off the ham before baking it?" The mother-in-law looked confused for a moment and then exclaimed, "Oh! That was the only way I could make it fit into my baking dish."

It's natural to do things the way we have seen them done, even if we don't know or understand the reasons behind them. Even Jesus did things the way His Father did them. But unlike us, He did them knowing full well the reason behind them all: to give us eternal life.

Consider the breath of God. Scripture begins "in the beginning," with God creating all things (Genesis 1:1). He created man from the dust of the ground, and that is all we were—dust. We were dry and frail until God breathed life into us (Genesis 2:7). Not until God's breath entered our lungs did we become fully alive. We were handmade, but we were *breathed* into existence. We see the power of God's breath again in the valley of dry bones (Ezekiel 37:4–5). In that valley the breath of God brought those dry bones back to life. It was the garden of Eden all over again. New breath. New life. And remember, Jesus was with God from the beginning: He saw all that His Father did.

Now, after Jesus' death, His disciples must have felt incredibly weary and worn. Their spirits were no doubt dry, and their faith more than a little frail. It was the perfect time for Jesus the Son to do exactly what He had seen God the Father do. And so Jesus did.

The men were gathered in that Upper Room. The doors were locked. Everyone was frightened. Jesus entered the room and it happened: He *breathed* on them! When Jesus breathed, the disciples were given the amazing gift of the Holy Spirit. They were given new energy to go out into the world and continue the work of God. New breath. New life.

Do you ever feel as though the trials and struggles of life have sucked the breath right out of you? Do you find yourself feeling a little dry? Do you long to feel fully alive again? No vitamin regimen or diet plan can bring dry bones to life. No commitment to become more organized can breathe life back into your world.

Only God has the life-restoring, spirit-refreshing, body energizing kind of breath you need. And it's found in His Word. Take the time to open the pages of Scripture and allow God to breathe life back into you. It's what He has done from the very beginning.

DAY 37

Doubting Thomas

The other disciples told him, "We have seen the Lord!" But he said to them, "Unless I see the nail marks in his hands and put my finger where the nails were, and put my hand into his side, I will not believe."

—JOHN 20:25

How quick are you to believe people? I used to believe anything and everything, and the people around me had a good time with it. Let's just say that there was a period of time in my childhood when I believed that my mother sat up all night poking the holes in my Cheerios.

Some things we don't really need to see for ourselves in order to believe. For instance, we can live productive lives never seeing, but still believing, that the largest chocolate bunny was sculpted in South Africa and stood over twelve feet tall.

Other things are a little harder to fully grasp without seeing them. If you've ever been to see a Ripley's Believe It or Not! exhibit, you know there are countless people, places, and things that you would almost *have* to see for yourself to believe.

Some people just need to see to believe—people like Thomas. The last time Thomas saw Jesus, He was hanging on a cross. Jesus had cried, "It is finished," and it all seemed, well, *finished*. So when the disciples told Thomas that they had seen the risen Lord, it was more than Thomas could comprehend. It's tempting to judge and say that he should have believed; after all, the others were convinced. But remember, they had seen Jesus with their own eyes! He had walked into the Upper Room, stood among them, and breathed on them, for crying out loud!

Don't you love that Jesus didn't leave Thomas in doubt? A week after first appearing to the disciples, Jesus came back again. This time, though, Thomas was there in the room. He was invited to see the scarred hands of Christ with his own eyes, to reach out and touch His side. Then Thomas believed.

We haven't had the privilege of seeing Christ with our own eyes. We will one day, and it will be more than our minds can comprehend. But we don't have to wait until that day to believe. As Jesus told Thomas, "Blessed are those who have not seen and yet have believed" (John 20:29).

Believe. When the world wants you to doubt, don't give in to it. Be among those who have not seen and yet have believed.

Forgive me, Lord, for the times I have doubted. Teach me to *believe* and trust You in every situation.

We Walk by Faith and Not by Sight

We walk by faith, and not by sight;
No gracious words we hear
From Him who spake as man e'er spake;
But we believe Him near.
—from "We Walk by Faith and Not by Sight"
by Henry Alford (1844)

The poetry in today's hymn reminds us that, yes, there will be times when we can't hear Jesus speaking. When we can't see Him. When we, like Thomas, doubt. These times are unavoidable. But what can we do in reaction?

Take the time to read or sing through the full text of Henry Alford's old hymn, and reflect on the way he frames our responses to God. We believe, we cry out, we rejoice, we seek—and finally, one day, we behold Him. Our Enemy would love it if we reacted to our blindness, deafness, and unbelief by withdrawing in shame. But today we are reminded that that doesn't have to be the case! Our Savior is more than merciful enough to bring us through. As Jesus offered His side and hands to doubting Thomas, He responds to our cries for help with His power, in His time. We don't see Him, but we know He's there.

DAY 39

Easter Baskets

Jesus said this to indicate the kind of
death by which Peter would glorify God.
Then he said to him, "Follow me!"
—JOHN 21:19

How do you feel about Peeps? You know, the chick-shaped marshmallow concoctions that seem to have the shelf life of a sweet forever? And don't even get me started on the chocolate eggs with the much-too-realistic yolk center. With all the things that go in them, Easter baskets have become a fun, delicious, and slightly wacky tradition. When the Easter bunny first arrived in America in the 1700s, he initially left only colored eggs. But as the tradition spread, he began leaving candy and gifts as well. Some may question the whole concept of Easter baskets and presents, but Scripture tells us that the risen Christ set the precedent by giving a much bigger gift to Peter.

Following the Last Supper, Jesus predicted that Peter was going to deny Him—and Peter was emphatic that such a thing would never take place. No, he would never do that! He could

not fathom turning his back on Jesus, let alone verbally denying that he even knew his Lord. And while Peter took all the heat for going back on his word in that scenario, the fact is that all of the other disciples said the same. They all claimed to be willing to die with Jesus, yet only one disciple—John—was present at the cross (John 19:26).

So, we have Peter saying he would never disown Jesus—with the result being absolute shame when that's exactly what Peter did. Following Peter's denial, everything escalated very quickly when Jesus was arrested. The mobs were yelling. There were beatings, nails, and a cross. The disciples scattered. The people mocked. Everything was chaotic and out of control. And then Jesus was dead and buried in a tomb. There was no chance to make things right. There was no taking back the denial. Peter must have been devastated.

Following such a shameful and public failing, Peter went back to what he knew. He returned to fishing. Perhaps, as he sat in the boat, he replayed in his mind the years spent with Jesus. All we know is that when John recognized the resurrected Jesus and said, "It is the Lord!" Peter dove right into the water (John 21:7). The others may have been willing to row to shore, but Peter didn't have time for that. He had to get to Jesus.

After a conversation in which Peter declared his love for the Savior, Jesus offered him an Easter gift. It came in the form of the very same command that began it all years before when Jesus first called the disciples. Jesus stood before Peter and said, "Follow me" (v. 19). It was the gift of a new beginning. It was the assurance and the reassurance that Peter could still be used by His Lord.

The gift of Easter is that Christ's mercy sees beyond our failings and loves beyond our shame. Our pasts do not render us useless in the hands of God. Our mistakes do not cancel His mission to seek and save. As you see the small gifts and sweet tokens tucked into Easter baskets this year, remember the much larger gift you've been given: redemption. Let go of the lies that say you've messed up one too many times. Resolve to accept the Easter offering and choose to follow Him.

Pineapple Upside-Down Cake

*"He himself bore our sins" in his body
on the cross, so that we might die to
sins and live for righteousness; "by his
wounds you have been healed."*

—1 PETER 2:24

The pineapple upside-down cake is a popular Easter dessert at our house. The amazing thing about this cake is that the sweetest, gooiest part stays hidden until the very end. For most cakes, you fill your pan with the cake batter first and then place all the pretties on top. But that's not at all how this dessert goes down. The cherries and pineapples are hidden in the bottom of the pan and completely covered by the cake batter. It enters the oven looking plain and ordinary. Only after it has been baked, removed from the pan, and completely turned upside down is its beauty (and deliciousness) fully known.

Living as a Christ-follower works much the same way. So often life looks plain and ordinary—at least in the beginning. Just as the disciples were baffled by a Messiah who would kneel

to wash their feet, we are faced with a world that often works contrary to the way we think it should. In her book *One Thousand Gifts*, Ann Voskamp calls this the "fundamental, lavish, radical nature of the upside-down economy of God."[1]

Everything is upside-down in Christ's commandments. The first will be last, and the last will be first (Matthew 19:30). Love your enemy (Matthew 5:44). Turn the other cheek to the one who strikes you (Matthew 5:39). Nothing says "upside-down" like Easter. Christ's wounds healed us, and the grave held the key to eternal life.

It's tempting to look at this broken world and think there is no beauty in it. And maybe it does appear a little plain and ordinary. It's possible that nothing is as you thought it would be. Right now, we see "through a glass, darkly"—glimpsing only a part of God's big picture (1 Corinthians 13:12 KJV).

Be brave enough to persevere in life—through the plain and ordinary, even the downright icky. There *will* come a day when everything that's upside-down gets flipped right-side up. God will reveal the beauty that was there all along but we just couldn't see. We will know fully, we will see clearly, and we will be with Jesus for eternity—and it will be so very sweet.

You call me to live *differently* from the world, Lord. Give me the grace and *wisdom* to do it well and remind me of my hope in You.

Notes

Day 1: No Turning Back
Andreas J. Köstenberger and Justin Taylor, *The Final Days of Jesus* (Wheaton, IL: Crossway, 2014), 32.

Day 7: The Old Rugged Cross
Quoted in Robert J. Morgan, *Then Sings My Soul, Book 3* (Nashville: Thomas Nelson, 2011), 217.

Day 19: That's My King
There are plenty of places online where you can hear Lockridge himself deliver his Detroit 1976 sermon. You can find an excerpt from Grace Community Church, "That's My King" by SM Lockridge, Vimeo.com, accessed July 28, 2016, https://vimeo.com/66414021.

Day 20: The Choice
"G987 - blasphēmeō – Strong's Greek Lexicon (KJV)." *Blue Letter Bible.* https://www.blueletterbible.org//lang/lexicon/lexicon.cfm?Strongs =G987&t=KJV.

Day 22: A Taste of Vinegar

David Mathis, "The Wine Jesus Drank," (May 27, 2010). http://www
.desiringgod.org/articles/the-wine-jesus-drank.

Day 26: Sunday's Comin'

This is an excerpt from Lockridge's "That's My King" sermon,
(1976), readily available in several places online (including YouTube,
uploaded by Keith Brown, January 31, 2012, https://www.youtube.com
/watch?v=4BhI4JKACUs). Here is a dramatized excerpt of the famous
"Friday" section, uploaded to YouTube by PastorRufus1, April 6, 2012,
https://www.youtube.com/watch?v=8gx6_rGLz20.

Day 29: Sweet Friendship

Tara Parker-Pope, "What Are Friends For? A Longer Life," *New York
Times,* April 20, 2009, http://www.nytimes.com/2009/04/21/health
/21well.html?_r=0.

Day 31: Christ the Lord Is Risen Today!

Scott P. Richert, "Why Don't Roman Catholics Sing the Alleluia
During Lent?" *About Religion,* February 23, 2015, http://catholicism
.about.com/od/worship/f/No_Alleluia.htm.

Day 40: Pineapple Upside-Down Cake

Ann Voskamp, *One Thousand Gifts: A Dare to Live Fully Right Where
You Are* (Grand Rapids: Zondervan, 2010), 197.